Neervoort J. R. H. Van De Poll

Monographical Essay on the Australian buprestid genus

Astraeus C. et G

Neervoort J. R. H. Van De Poll

Monographical Essay on the Australian buprestid genus Astraeus C. et G

ISBN/EAN: 9783337851880

Printed in Europe, USA, Canada, Australia, Japan

Cover: Foto ©Andreas Hilbeck / pixelio.de

More available books at **www.hansebooks.com**

MONOGRAPHICAL ESSAY

ON THE

AUSTRALIAN BUPRESTID GENUS ASTRAEUS C. ET G.

BY

J. R. H. NEERVOORT VAN DE POLL.

———

Although only two years have elapsed since I published a synopsis of the genus *Astraeus* with descriptions of three new species, now I am already able to treble the number of the known species and to carry it up to nineteen. This great amount of new material is partly due to the acquisitions I made successively of the Buprestid collections of Mr. E. W. Janson, Mr. Th. von Demuth and Dr. F. Baden; each of these collections enriched my set of *Astraeus* with interesting novelties. However, for the knowledge of the greater part of the new species I am indebted to the rich series of *Astraeus* my friend Mr. R. Oberthür placed most courteously into my hands for the purpose of this study. The Interior and the West coast of Australia becoming the more and more explored, we may still expect the discovery of a good number of new species. As the great similarity in pattern of the greater part of the species, makes it very difficult to identify these insects with certainty (as yet I never received a collection, wherein they were correctly named), I thought it useful to illustrate this paper with colored figures of all the species, and I have been fortunate enough to secure for this laboursome work the able pencil of the well known Natural History painter Mr. J. Migneaux.

History of the Genus.

The genus *Astraeus* has been established in 1837 by Mrs. Laporte and Gory in behalf of a new insect, which they described under the name of *Astraeus flavopictus*. This species remained for a long time the only representative of the genus. In 1857 Mr. Lacordaire published in his standard work « *Genera des Coléoptères* » an excellent generic description, but it was not before 1868 that Mr. E. Saunders, giving full descriptions of the unrecognizable diagnoses of the Australian Buprestidae described by the Rev. Hope [1]), made known that *Stigmodera Samouelli* Hope belongs to the genus *Astraeus*. The Munich Catalogue (1869) enumerates these two species only, but the Catalogus Buprestidarum (1871) of Mr. E. Saunders contains still a third species, viz. *Astraeus navarchis* Thoms. This species had been described already in 1856, but Thomson, having over-looked the existance of a genus *Astraeus*, placed his insect in the genus *Conognathus* and there it remained unrecognized for so long a period. Two years afterwards (1873) the second volume of the *Trans. of the Ent. Soc. of N. S. Wales* contained the description (N.B. the description was read 4th December 1871) of *Astraeus Mastersi* Mc L.; this species, however, proves to be merely a variety of *A. Samouelli*. In this state I found the genus, as I attempted two years ago (1886) to contribute to its knowledge by publishing a synopsis and the descriptions of three new species and two varieties, viz. *Astraeus aberrans*, *elongatus*, *pygmaeus* with the var. *subfasciatus* and the var. *dilutipes* of *A. Samouelli*. There remained some errors in my publication, which were caused firstly, as I knew *A. navarchis* from description only, and secondly by mistaking a still undescribed species for *A. flavopictus*, which might find its excuse in the great similarity of the pattern on the elytra of both the species and chiefly in the misleading circumstance, that Castelnau and Gory designed the elytral sculpture as « élytres

---

1) After discussion which is reported in *Proc. Ent. Soc.*, 1867, pp. cix, cx, it has been settled, that Mr. Hope's paper was printed only for private circulation and therefore it must be regarded as an unpublished tract.

striées, ponctuées », whilst in fact the sculpture consists of sharp ridges. Also having now more specimens of my var. *dilutipes*, I have raised it to the rank of a distinct species. Finally no one will wonder, I suppose, that an arrangement made for six species proves to be quite inapplicable for nineteen species.

List of Works quoted.

Gemminger, Dr., et Harold, B. de, Catalogus Coleopterorum. Tom. V (1869).

Hope, F. W., Buprestidae (1836), (printed only for private circulation).

Lacordaire, J. Th., Suites à Buffon, Coléoptères, IV (1857).

Laporte, F. L. de, et Gory, H., Histoire Naturelle et Iconographie des Coléoptères. Monographie des Buprestides, (1835—41).

Mac Leay, W., Notes on a Collection of Insects from Gayndah. (*Trans. Ent. Soc. of N. S. Wales*, II, 1873).

Poll, J. R. H. Neervoort van de, Description of three new species and a Synopsis of the Buprestid genus *Astraeus* C. and G. (*Not. from the Leyd. Mus.*, VIII, 1886).

Saunders, E., Revision of the Australian Buprestidae described by the Rev. F. H. Hope. (*Trans. Ent. Soc. of Lond.*, for the year 1868).

—— Catalogus Buprestidarum (1871).

Thomson, J., Description de dix Coléoptères. (*Rev. et Mag. de Zool.*, VIII, 1856).

Generic Characteristics and Classification.

I have made already allusion to the excellent explanation of the generic characteristics in Prof. Lacordaire's classical work, however, as his description is taken from a single species, some of the characters are too restricted and ought to become somewhat more extensive, in order to be not in contradiction with specific differences, which a so much larger number of species necessarily afford.

Head plain, generally of moderate size, occasionally large; epistoma very short, broadly semicircularly emarginated; labrum transverse, slightly incised; antennary cavities small and rounded; eyes large, widely separated on the vertex. Antennae of variable length and shape, rather long and slender, in some species very long; sometimes hardly, sometimes distinctly serrated; 1st joint long, thickened at the top, 2nd very small, obconic, 3rd slightly longer than the following, the remainder almost of equal length, flattened, more or less broadened at the apices.

Prothorax transverse, convex, rounded at the sides, narrowed towards the top, very deeply notched on both sides at the base, with the median lobe and the hinder angles strongly projecting and pointed.

Scutellum invisible.

Elytra rather convex, broadly bi-lobated at the base, the lobes acutely produced and overreaching the base of the thorax, gradually narrowed towards the top, diverging at the suture; the apex of each ending in a strong sharp point, formed by a lateral emargination, which forms also a strong, rarely an obsolete, lateral tooth; enlarged below the shoulders, the dilatation sometimes short and rounded, sometimes long and angular, covering a small part of the breast.

Legs rather robust; tarsi long and slender, the first joint long, sometimes almost as long as the other joints together.

Metasternum broadly but shallowly emarginated; mesosternum short; prosternum broad, flat, rarely somewhat convex or concave.

General shape rather convex, gradually narrowed anteriorly and chiefly posteriorly.

In the memoir, I published two years ago, I have arranged the few species known at that time in two groups, according to the shape of the humeral dilatation of the elytra. The knowledge of a larger number of species proves, however, that this characteristic is quite unsatisfactory to arrange them according to their true affinities; although the shape of that humeral dilatation remains of great interest for specific distinction, it is useless for dividing the species into groups. The great similarity in sculpture, color and position of the spots, and the absence of well defined peculiarities, make the arrangement of the greater part of the species a very puzzling task, and I have had a good deal of trouble, before obtaining a somewhat satisfactory tabulation. I have divided the material into two principal groups, which I shall indicate as «A s t r a c i a b e r r a n t e s» and «A s t r a c i v e r i»; the former contains only four species, whilst the latter includes all the remainder. In the group of the «Astraci veri» I have included all the species presenting the typical shape of *Astraeus*, having the top of the elytra strongly diverging and ending in a strong sharp point, and also provided with a strong lateral tooth; the elytral sculpture of all the species consists in sharp ridges. The group of the «Astraci aberrantes» has the elytra hardly diverging, ending in short, rather blunt apical-points, moreover there is hardly any lateral emargination and consequently no, or, as in one case, only a short lateral tooth; the elytra are punctate-striate with the interstices punctured or transversely rugose. This group might be split into two divisions, each containing two species. The species of the first division bear a strong resemblance with some *Buprestis (Ancylocheira)*-species and chiefly the new *Astraeus lineatus* could be easily mistaken for the American *Buprestis lineata* F. The species of the second division are more different in outline, as well from the first division as from the Astraei veri; they are heavy-bodied, parallel-sided and not much narrowed anteriorly and posteriorly, wanting the characteristic slender shape of the more typical Astraci. However, these two species are exactly the connecting links between the first division of the aberrant Astraci on one side and the true Astraci on the other side, one of the species having no trace of a lateral tooth, whilst the other presents a distinct one.

Synopsis of Species.

I. Apices of elytra slightly diverging, without or with a short lateral tooth. Elytra punctate-striate: Astraci aberrantes.

A. Elytral interstices sparingly punctured.

　　1. Elytra ornated with large and small
　　　　irregular spots . . . . *irregularis* v. d. Poll.

　　2. Elytra ornated ·with four broad
　　　　longitudinal stripes. . . . . . . *lineatus* v. d. Poll.

B. Elytral interstices strongly transversely
　　rugose.

　　3. Elytra ornated with numerous
　　　　punctiform spots . . . . *multinotatus* v. d. Poll.

　　4. Elytra ornated with numerous
　　　　strigiform spots. . . . . *aberrans* v. d. Poll.

II. Apices of elytra strongly diverging, with
　　a strong lateral tooth. Elytra costate:
　　Astraei veri.

　A. Legs unicolor.

　a. Broad species.

　　α. Elytra with a transverse band before
　　　　and an other below the middle.

　　　* Elytral costae obsolete.

　　5. Large species; band before the
　　　　middle touching the suture . . *navarchis* Thoms.

　　** Elytral costae sharp.

　　6. Small species; band before the
　　　　middle not touching the suture. *fraterculus* v. d. Poll.

　　7. Elytra with an additional small spot
　　　　at the base and an other before
　　　　the apex . . . . *Badeni* v. d. Poll.

　　β. Elytra with a sutural and a lateral
　　　　row of irregular spots.

　　　* Elytral costae sharp.

　　8. Small species; sutural row of 5,
　　　　lateral row of 3 spots; the 4th
　　　　sutural and the 3rd lateral placed
　　　　abreast . . . . *Jansoni* v. d. Poll.

　　　** Elytral costae obsolete.

9. Large species; sutural row of 4 or
   5, lateral row of 3 spots; the 3rd
   lateral placed between the 3rd
   and 4th sutural spot . . . . . *crassus* v. d. Poll.

b. Slender species.

α. Head of normal size.

* Apical spots of the sutural and
  lateral row strigiform; the lateral
  row partly or entirely confluent.

10. Sutural row of 4 spots. Thorax
    normal . . . . *flavopictus* C. and G.

11. Sutural row of 3 spots. Thorax
    conically elevated. . . . . . . *prothoracicus* v. d. Poll.

12. Sutural row of spots confluent,
    forming a broad longitudinal
    stripe. Thorax normal. . . . . *vittatus* v. d. Poll.

** Apical spots rounded. The lateral
   spots widely separated.

13. Each elytron with an oblique fascia
    before the middle, one basal and
    three postmedian spots . . . . *Oberthüri* v. d. Poll.

β. Head unusual large.

14. Elytra with a sutural row of 4 and
    a lateral row of 3 spots. . . . *elongatus* v. d. Poll.

B. Legs partly testaceous.

a. Head without frontal carina.

15. Each elytron with a broad fascia
    before and an other below the
    middle, a large basal and a very
    small apical spot. . . . . . . *simulator* v. d. Poll.

b. Head with a frontal carina.

16. Each elytron with 4 spots. (Some-
    times the subhumeral spot is
    confluent with the submedian
    spot, var. *subfasciatus* m.) . . *pygmaeus* v. d. Poll.

17. Each elytron with 5 spots. . . . *dilutipes* v. d. Poll.

18. Same pattern as the preceding,
     but with an additional small spot
     just at the shoulder edge, and
     the subhumeral spot evidently
     composed of two confluent spots.
     (Sometimes the subhumeral spot
     is confluent with the submedian
     spot, var. *Mastersi* Mac Leay). *Samouelli* Saund.

19. Each elytron with a very broad
     fascia before and an other below
     the middle, a large basal and a
     small apical spot. . . . . *splendens* v. d. Poll.

DESCRIPTION OF SPECIES.

(The numbers of the descriptions correspond with the numbers
of the figures on plate II and III).

1. Astraeus irregularis v. d. Poll. — nov. spec.

Supra niger, nitidus, capite elytrisque cyaneo-internitentibus; capite prothoraceque nonnullis maculis parvis, singulis elytris ad basin maculis parvis, ante medium macula magna subrotundata, apicem versus macula magna longitudinali et nonnullis maculis parvis, flavis ornatis. Subtus obscure viridi-aeneus; segmentis omnibus ad latera gutta, sterno maculis pluribus parvis, flavis notatis; pedibus rubris, subaenescentibus. Caput crassum, confertim punctatum. Prothorax modice convexus, lateribus apicem versus subrotundato-angustatis; fortiter denseque punctatus, ad latera rugosus. Elytra striato-punctata, interstitiis planis, sparsim, lateraliter sat dense punctatis; apicibus paullo divergentibus, spinis marginalibus deficientibus. Pars infera crebre punctata, pubescentia sericea induta; prosterno subconcavo.

Long. 13 mm., lat. 4½ mm.

Habitat: Australia.

Head nitid black, with a dark cyaneous tinge, somewhat greenish
in front, with three yellow spots around each eye, an elongated

spot in front and two punctiform spots on the vertex. Prothorax
black, less shining, with two yellow spots at the front-margin,
below these two other ones before the base and three small spots
along the sides. Elytra black with a dark bluish hue, shining;
each elytron ornated with the following yellow markings, viz.
three irregular small spots at the base, an other small one below
the shoulder, a very large transverse spot before the middle, below
the middle an irregular stripe close to the outer margin and not
reaching the apex, and two small spots near the suture. Underside
dark aeneous green, very shining; the breast with six yellow spots
in the middle and three on each side; all the abdominal segments
with a yellow blotch laterally, these blotches becoming gradually
smaller towards the apex. Legs red with a bronzy tinge.

Head large, swollen, closely punctured, more finely on the
vertex, between the eyes a short glabrous line. Prothorax strongly
and coarsely punctured, towards the sides slightly rugose, the
median lobe with a small impression; slightly convex, the sides
rounded and somewhat narrowed towards the top. Elytra striated,
the striae composed of transversely impressed large shallow oblong
punctures, the interstices plain, sparingly punctured, more strongly
along the sides; rather parallel-sided, strongly narrowed behind
the middle, the apices slightly diverging, each of them ending in
a strong tooth. Beneath coarsely but minutely punctured, the
median portion of the breast with a few scattered punctures only;
clothed, legs included, with a silvery pubescence, chiefly along
the sides; prosternum somewhat concave.

Variability. The pattern being already different on both the
elytra of the single specimen, I have at my disposal, we may
conclude a great variability of the yellow markings; the basal and
apical spots have a tendency to flow together.

Unique in coll. Oberthür.

2. **Astraeus lineatus** v. d. Poll. — nov. spec.

*Supra niger, nitidus, purpureo- vel viridi-aeneo-internitens; pro-
thorace lateraliter linea, ad basin maculis duabus singulis, elytris*

lineis latis irregularibus duabus rubris vel flavis ornatis. Subtus purpureo-cupreus, sterno segmentisque abdominis lateraliter maculis rubris notatis, pedibus viridi-aeneis. Omnino pubescentia sericea obtectus, densissime in abdomine, minutissime in elytris. Caput crebre rugoso-punctatum, in medio linea glabra. Prothorax subconvexus, lateribus rectis, apicem versus angustatis; confertim punctatus, ad latera rugosus. Elytra striato-punctata; interstitiis subconvexis, sparsim punctatis, subtilissime transversaliter plicatis; apicibus paullo divergentibus, spinis marginalibus deficientibus. Pars infera dense punctata; prosterno paullisper concavo.

Long. 11—14 mm., lat. 4—5 mm.

Habitat: N. W. Australia.

Uppersurface shining black with a purplish or bronzy-green reflection, chiefly on the forehead; head with two reddish spots underneath the eyes, prothorax bordered with a narrow reddish stripe along the sides and with a spot of the same color on each side of the median lobe; each of the elytra ornated with two broad irregular reddish stripes, one close to the suture, originating at the base and nearly reaching the apex, and the other commencing below the shoulder, where it touches the margin, then continuing at some distance along the outer margin, ending close to the sutural stripe. Undersurface and legs purplish-coppery, the breast marked laterally with two reddish spots, the abdominal segments with a spot on each side, these spots becoming very small on the three last segments. Above sparingly covered with a short silvery pile, beneath thickly clothed with the silvery pubescence.

Head strongly rugosely punctured, with a short glabrous line in front. Prothorax slightly convex, sides almost straight, obliquelly narrowed towards the top, thickly punctured, rugose at the sides. Elytra with rather prominent shoulders, slightly diverging at the suture, apices ending in short spines; striate-punctate, the interstices subconvex, sparingly punctured and faintly strigose in a transverse direction. Beneath closely punctured, the punctures being coarsest on the prosternum and finest on the abdomen; prosternum somewhat concave.

Variability. In one specimen there is an additional reddish spot just above the epistoma. The elytral stripes are sometimes united at the top.

Number of specimens examined: three, in coll. Oberthür.

3. Astraeus multinotatus v. d. Poll. — nov. spec.

Robustus, supra niger subcoeruleo-internitens, capite thoraceque opacis, elytris nitidis; subtus cum pedibus atro-coeruleus, nitidus. Omnino maculis perparvis numerosis flavis notatus. Caput fortiter punctatum, in medio plaga glabra. Prothorax brevis, convexus, lateribus rotundatis, apicem versus multo angustatis, fortiter et creberrime punctatus, lateraliter punctis majoribus instructus. Elytra striata, interstitiis sat convexis, sparsim punctatis, transversaliter plicatis; post medium latiora, apicibus paullo divergentibus, spinis lateralibus deficientibus. Pars infera omnino confertim punctata.

Long. 15 mm., lat. 6 mm.

Habitat: N. W. Australia.

Robust; uppersurface black with bluish reflections, elytra shining, head and thorax rather dull; undersurface and legs cyaneous black, very shining. The whole body, thighs included, speckled with very minute yellow spots, underneath the spots are somewhat larger, and they are confluent on the abdominal segments.

Head coarsely punctured, with a small glabrous patch above between the eyes. Prothorax short, convex, sides strongly rounded and narrowed towards the top, hinder angles slightly bent inwards; deeply and closely punctured, strongest at the sides. Elytra broadest behind the middle, then suddenly narrowed towards the top, hardly diverging at the suture, apices ending in very short and blunt points; striated, the interstices rather convex, deeply punctured and sensibly plicated in a transverse direction, the sculpture being strongest near the apex and along the margins. Beneath coarsely punctured all over, the punctures at the sides of the prosternum very large.

The single specimen I have at my disposal, being old and rubbed, is entirely destitute of hairs; judging from analogy, fresh examples will be clothed partly with silvery pubescence.

Unique in coll. Oberthür.

4. Astraeus aberrans v. d. Poll.

Astraeus aberrans v. d. Poll, *Not. from the Leyd. Mus.*, VIII (1886), p. 176.

Robustus, supra niger, purpureo-internitens, nitidus, elytris plurimis maculis flavis strigiformibus ornatis. Subtus nitidus, obscure aeneus vel cupreus, duobus segmentis primis abdominis lateraliter pustula flava notatis. Omnino pubescentia sericea indutus, in elytris obsoletissime. Caput fortiter rugoso-punctatum. Prothorax convexus, brevis, lateribus rotundatis, apicem versus subangustatis; crebre punctatus, ad latera rugosus. Elytra profunde striata, interstitiis convexis, valde densissimeque transversaliter rugoso-striata, apicibus fere haud divergentibus, spinis suturalibus et marginalibus parvis. Pars infera crebre punctata.

var. nov. *picticollis* v. d. Poll. *A typo differt, prothorace maculis nonnullis flavis ornato.*

Long. 14—18 mm., lat. 6—7 mm.

Habitat: West-Australia, Swan River, Nicol-Bay.

Uppersurface black, with purplish reflections, the forehead and the sides of the thorax coppery, slightly shining, the elytra with numerous strigiform yellow spots, viz. a row close to the suture, an other row along the middle, overreaching the foregoing, one spot at the base between these rows and two spots above at the outer margin. Undersurface and legs dark bronzy, purple-brown or coppery, shining; the first two or three abdominal segments with a small round yellow spot at each side; rather thickly clothed with silvery pubescence.

Head strongly rugosely punctured, with a longitudinal glabrous line in the middle, hairy. Prothorax convex, short, the sides rounded, slightly narrowed towards the top and somewhat emarginate before the posterior angles; deeply punctured, rugose at the sides, hairy. Elytra broadest behind the middle, apices hardly diverging, the sutural and lateral spines very short and obtuse; deeply striated, the interstices almost equally elevated and rugosely striated in a transverse direction; covered with a delicate silvery pile. Underneath closely punctate, more finely on the abdomen.

Variability. The rows of strigiform spots are sometimes confluent, forming irregular stripes; in one specimen the yellow markings even extend on the disc and along the sides of the thorax (var. *picticollis* m.), and there are additional small spots at the margins of the elytra and on the fourth abdominal segment.

Number of specimens examined: nine, in coll. Oberthür and van de Poll.

5. Astraeus navarchis Thoms.

Conognathus navarchis Thoms., *Rev. et Mag. Zool.*, 1856, p. 115, pl. VI, fig. 2.

Astraeus navarchis v. d. Poll, *Not. from the Leyd. Mus.*, VIII (1886), p. 180.

Latus, nitidissimus, purpureus; elytris ante medium fascia flava suturam attingente, post medium fascia suturam haud attingente, ornatis. Caput rugoso-punctatum, inter oculos leviter excavatum. Prothorax brevissimus, convexus, lateribus rotundatis, apicem versus valde angustatis, angulis posticis multo prominulis; fortiter punctatus, densius in lateribus, in medio linea glabra longitudinali. Elytra subcostata (costae basin versus indistinctae), interstitiis basin versus subconvexis, sparsim punctatis; apicibus valde divergentibus, spinis suturalibus lateralibusque validis, acutis. Pars infera crebre punctata, subtilius in abdomine; prosterno subconvexo.

Long. 16—17 mm., lat. 6—7 mm.

Habitat: Australia.

Entirely of a bright metallic purple color, head and thorax rather darker, purple-brown. Each elytron with a slightly curved yellow band before the middle, touching the suture as well as the outer margin below the shoulder, its concavity turned towards the base, and an other somewhat angular band below the middle, which touches the margin but does not reach the suture.

Head rugosely punctured, slightly excavated between the eyes, with a sharp ridge in front. Prothorax very short and convex, the sides rounded and strongly narrowed towards the top, the posterior angles much projecting, narrowly margined along the front and the sides; deeply punctured, more coarsely at the sides, with a glabrous line in the middle and a small impression on the median lobe. Elytra strongly narrowed below the middle, apices strongly diverging, ending in very long and acute spines, the lateral spines also large and acute, the humeral fold acutely produced; subcostate, the costae only distinct near the apex, where the interstices are plain, whilst they become the more and more convex towards the base, each of the interstices with a row of large deeply impressed punctures. Beneath densely punctate, very finely and closely on the abdomen, clothed with extremely minute hairs; prosternum slightly convex.

Variability. In one specimen in rather bad condition and of an obscure aeneous color (perhaps the color is spoiled in bad alcohol), the yellow band before the middle turns its convexity instead of its concavity towards the base.

Number of specimens examined: three, in coll. Oberthür.

6. Astraeus fraterculus v. d. Poll. — nov. spec.

Latus, nitidissimus; supra atro-coerulens, elytris ante medium et post medium fascia flava suturam haud attingente, ornatis; subtus viridi-aeneus, pedibus violaceis. Caput sat dense punctatum, in medio linea glabra. Prothorax brevissimus, convexus, lateribus rotundatis, apicem versus valde angustatis, angulis posticis multo prominentibus; aequaliter punctatus. Elytra costata, interstitiis planis, indistincte punctatis et rugosis; apicibus valde divergentibus, spinis suturalibus marginalibusque validis, acutis. Pars infera confertim punctata, subtilius sed densissime in abdomine, prosterno subrugoso; pubescentia minutissima sericea induta.

Long. 10—11 mm., lat. 4½—5 mm.

Habitat: Victoria, King George's Sound.

Uppersurface bluish-black with violaceous or greenish reflections, very shining, underneath aeneous-green with the legs violaceous, shining. Each elytron with a curved yellow band before the middle , touching the outer margin below the shoulder but not reaching the suture, its concavity turned towards the base, and an other somewhat angular band below the middle, also touching the outer margin only.

Head regularly punctured, with an elevated line in front. Prothorax very short and convex, the sides strongly rounded and narrowed towards the top, the posterior angles much projecting, narrowly margined along the front and the sides; distinctly but sparsely punctured on the disc, somewhat more densely at the sides. Elytra strongly narrowed below the middle, apices strongly diverging, the sutural and lateral spines very long and acute, the humeral fold angularly not acutely produced, provided with sharp ridges, the interstices plain, faintly punctured and transversely wrinkled. Beneath coarsely punctured, more finely on the abdomen, the prosternum rather rugose; clothed with a delicate silvery pubescence.

This species is closely allied to the preceding, but besides the great difference in size and color, it may be easily distinguished by the elytral costae, which are distinct over the whole of their length.

Two specimens in coll. Oberthür.

7. Astraeus Badeni v. d. Poll. — nov. spec.

Latus, nitidus, supra niger, cyaneo- vel purpureo-internitens; elytris ante et post medium fascia flava suturam haud attingente, ad basin et ante apicem pustula flava, ornatis. Subtus obscure aeneus. Caput crebre punctatum. Prothorax convexus, lateribus rotundatis, apicem versus sat angustatis; fortiter denseque punctatus, subtilius in disco. Elytra costata, interstitiis sat fortiter punctatis et plicatis; apicibus valde divergentibus, spinis suturalibus lateralibusque validis, acutis. Pars infera densissime punctata, subtilius in abdomine. Caput, prothorax et pars infera pubescentia minuta sericea obtecta.

Long. 9—10 mm., lat. 3½—4½ mm.

Habitat: South Australia, Gawler, Swan River.

Shining, head and thorax bronzy-black, the latter with faint purplish tinges; elytra bluish-black with a violaceous reflection, undersurface and legs dark aeneous, more or less mixed with purplish-brown. Each of the elytra with a yellow spot at the base, a curved yellow band before the middle, touching the outer margin below the shoulder and stopping close to the suture, its concavity turned towards the base, a smaller band, which also touches the outer margin only, below the middle, and a small spot before the apex.

Head coarsely punctured, hairy. Prothorax short and convex, strongly rounded at the sides and narrowed towards the top, slightly margined along the front and the sides; thickly punctured, coarsest laterally, with a faint indication of an impressed median line, hairy. Elytra strongly narrowed below the middle, apices much diverging, sutural and marginal spines strong and acute, the humeral fold rather large, slightly angularly produced; costate, the interstices plain, each of them with a row of large deeply impressed punctures, moreover slightly wrinkled in a transverse direction. Underneath very closely punctured, more finely on the abdomen; clothed with a soft silvery pubescence.

Variability. The basal band is often interrupted in the middle. In some specimens the apical spots are wanting and in one example the apical band is also reduced and does not reach the outer margin.

Number of specimens examined: six, in coll. Oberthür and van de Poll. Dedicated to Dr. F. Baden.

8. Astraeus Jansoni v. d. Poll. — nov. spec.

Latus, nitidus, supra niger, atro-coeruleo- vel viridi-aeneo- inter-nitens, singulis elytris octonis maculis flavis ornatis; subtus obscure viridi-aeneus. Caput dense punctatum. Prothorax convexus, lateribus rotundatis, apicem versus sensim angustatis; crebre punctatus, sub-tilius in disco. Elytra costata, interstitiis planis, indistincte punc-tatis et rugosis; apicibus valde divergentibus, spinis suturalibus lateralibusque validis, acutis. Pars infera densissime punctata, sub-

tilius in abdomine. Caput, prothorax et pars infera pubescentia minutissima sericea induta.

Long. 8—9$\frac{1}{2}$ mm., lat. 3$\frac{1}{2}$—4 mm.

Habitat: Adelaide, Gawler, Kangeroo Isl.

Shining, head and thorax bronzy-green, the latter with strong violaceous reflections, elytra black with a cyaneous, violaceous or bronzy-green hue; underneath and legs dark bronzy-green. Each of the elytra ornated with eight yellow spots, viz. a row of five spots along the suture, the first at the base, the second before the middle, the third and smallest just in the middle, the fourth below the middle and the fifth close to the apex, and a row of three spots at the outer margin, the first occupying the shoulder edge, the second opposite the interval between the 2nd and 3rd sutural spot and the third placed abreast with the 4th sutural one.

Head coarsely punctured, hairy. Prothorax convex, rather short, sides strongly rounded and narrowed towards the top, indistinctly bordered along the front and lateral margins; deeply punctured, the punctures becoming larger and almost confluent at the sides; hairy. Elytra strongly narrowed below the middle, apices rather strongly diverging, armed with long and acute sutural and marginal spines, the humeral fold large, broadly rounded; costate, the interstices plain, shallowly punctured and transversely wrinkled. Undersurface closely punctured, very minutely on the abdomen; clothed with a delicate silvery pile.

Variability. The central yellow spots of the sutural row have a tendency to disappear. I have, however, not yet seen a specimen in which they are entirely absent, but in one specimen the central spot is present on the right elytron only.

Number of specimens examined: ten, in coll. Oberthür and van de Poll. Dedicated to Mr. E. W. Janson.

9. Astraeus crassus v. d. Poll.

Astraeus flavopictus v. d. Poll, *Not. from the Leyd. Mus.*, VIII (1886), p. 180.

Latus, nitidissimus, supra purpureo-fuscus, subtus dilutius cupreo-

nitens; elytris singulis octonis vel novenis maculis flavis ornatis. Caput rugoso-punctatum, in medio longitudinaliter carinatum. Prothorax convexus, lateribus rotundatis, apicem versus sensim angustatis; fortiter punctatus et rugosus in lateribus. Elytra subcostata (costae basin versus indistinctae), interstitiis basin versus subconvexis, parce punctatis; apicibus valde divergentibus, spinis suturalibus marginalibusque validis, acutis. Pars infera creberrime punctata, subtilissime in abdomine. Caput, prothorax et pars infera pubescentia sericea induta.

Long. 12—17 mm., lat. 4½—7 mm.

Habitat: N. S. Wales, Port Denison, Brisbane.

Uppersurface brightly shining purple-brown, the thorax generally greenish on the disc, underneath and legs of a more brilliant coppery color. Each of the elytra ornated with eight irregular yellow spots, viz. a row of five spots close to the suture, gradually diminishing in size towards the apex, the first at the base, the second before the middle, the third below the middle, the fourth about midway between the foregoing and the apex, the fifth just before the sutural spine, and a row of three spots at the outer margin, placed opposite to the three intervals between the first four sutural spots, the subhumeral spot emitting a branch to the base.

Head rugosely punctured, with an elevated longitudinal line in front; hairy. Prothorax short and convex, sides strongly rounded and narrowed towards the top, indistinctly margined along the front and the sides; very deeply and confluently punctured on the disc, strongly rugose at the sides; hairy. Elytra suddenly narrowed below the middle, apices strongly diverging, the sutural and marginal spines strong and acute, the humeral fold broadly rounded; subcostate, the costae only distinct near the apex, according to the interstices, which become the more and more convex towards the base, each of the interstices with a row of distant shallow punctures. Beneath very closely punctate, the punctuation finest on the abdomen; clothed with a silvery pubescence.

Variability. The small apical spots are as often absent as

they are present; the branch which is emitted by the subhumeral spot is often separated; some specimens show unsymetrical additional spots, chiefly between the third and fourth sutural spots.

Number of specimens examined: eleven, in coll. Oberthür and van de Poll.

10. Astraeus flavopictus Cast. et Gory.

Astraeus flavopictus Cast. et Gory, *Mon.*, 1, *Astr.*, p. 2, pl. 1, fig. 1.

Elongatus, nitidus, supra purpureo-brunneus, elytris singulis maculis septenis flavis ornatis (maculae apicales strigiformes); subtus cupreo-aureus. Caput creberrime punctatum. Prothorax subconvexus, lateribus rotundatis, apicem versus mediocriter angustatis, fortiter punctatus, in lateribus rubrugosus. Elytra costata, interstitiis planis, regulariter punctatis et transversaliter plicatis; apicibus mediocriter divergentibus, spinis suturalibus lateralibusque sub-obtusis. Pars infera confertim punctata, in abdomine subtilius densiusque. Caput, prothorax et pars infera pubescentia densa sericea obtecta.

Long. 10—14 mm., lat. 4—5¼ mm.

Habitat: West Australia.

Uppersurface shining, purple-brown, the elytra more brilliant with a golden or violaceous reflection, underneath and legs golden coppery. Each elytron with seven yellow spots, viz. a row of four spots close to the suture, the first at the base, the second, a large transverse spot, before the middle, the third and smallest one just below the middle, the fourth, a strigiform spot, originating near the foregoing and stopping close to the apex, and a row of three spots at the outer margin, the first two of which are placed opposite to the intervals between the first three spots of the sutural row, the third, an elongated spot, almost abreast with the last sutural one, but much shorter; the subhumeral spot emits a branch to the base.

Head very closely punctured; hairy. Prothorax subconvex, the sides gently rounded and narrowed towards the top: deeply and thickly punctured, rugose at the sides; hairy. Elytra gradually narrowed towards the apex, apices not much divergent, sutural and lateral spines rather short and obtuse, the humeral fold moderately developed, angularly produced; costate, interstices plain, each of them with a row of large punctures, which become rather confluent near the base, moreover slightly wrinkled in a transverse direction. Beneath densely punctate, the sculpture being, however, indistinct according to the close silvery white pile, which covers the whole of the undersurface, legs included.

Variability. The strigiform sutural spots are often united with the foregoing spot and the three marginal spots are also sometimes confluent. There is one specimen with the head and thorax of an abnormal clear green color.

Number of specimens examined: eleven (including the original type of Castelnau and Gory, now in Mr. Oberthür's possession), in coll. Oberthür and van de Poll.

11. Astraeus prothoracicus v. d. Poll. — nov. spec.

Elongatus, nitidus, supra niger, capite prothoraceque viridi- aeneo-, elytris violaceo-internitentibus, singulis elytris maculis ternis (macula apicalis valde elongata) et linea laterali flavis ornatis. Subtus obscure viridi-metallicus, pedibus rubris. Caput crebre sed leviter punctatum. Prothorax in medio ad basin valde conice elevatus, lateribus rotundatis, apicem versus tantillum angustatis; confertim rugoso-punctatus. Elytra costata, interstitiis planis, regulariter punctatis, sat distincte transversaliter plicatis; apicibus mediocriter divergentibus, spinis suturalibus marginalibusque sub-obtusis. Pars infera crebre punctata, in abdomine subtilissime densissimeque.

Long. 10—11 mm., lat. 3½—4 mm.

Habitat: Clarence River, Champion Bay.

Shining, head and thorax dark aeneous green, elytra black with violaceous reflections, each of them with a flavous border, originating at the shoulder and occupying two thirds of the entire length and with three yellow spots along the suture, the first just at the base, the second before the middle and the third, a large elongate one, midway between the foregoing and the apex. Beneath dark bronzy-green, shining, legs red.

Head thickly but finely punctured; hairy. Prothorax convex, in the middle, just before the median lobe, strongly conically elevated, sides gently rounded and slightly narrowed towards the top; densely rugosely punctate, strigose on the elevated part; hairy. Elytra gradually narrowed towards the top, apices not strongly divergent, sutural and marginal spines rather short and obtuse, humeral fold rather small, angularly produced; costate, interstices plain, moderately transversely wrinkled and with a row of large distant punctures on each. Underneath coarsely punctured, the abdomen much more finely and densely; entirely clothed, legs included, with a dense silvery pubescence.

Two specimens in coll. Oberthür.

12. Astraeus vittatus v. d. Poll. — nov. spec.

Nitidus, supra niger, capite prothoraceque sub-aenescentibus, elytris obscure violaceis; singula elytra ad latera vitta flava angusta et in medio vitta lata irregulari ornata; subtus obscure purpureo-brunneus, pedibus rubris. Caput confertim punctatum. Prothorax subconvexus, lateribus apicem versus subrotundato-angustatis; profunde punctatus, subtilius in disco. Elytra costata, interstitiis planis, punctatis, paululum plicatis; apicibus mediocriter divergentibus, spinis suturalibus marginalibusque brevibus. Pars infera densissime minutissimeque punctata. Caput, thorax et pars infera pubescentia densa sericea induta.

Long. 10 mm., lat. 4 mm.

Habitat: N. W. Australia.

Shining; head and thorax black with purplish reflections, the latter bronzy-green in the middle, the elytra dark violaceous, each of them with a broad, somewhat irregular yellow stripe close to the suture, originating at the base and stopping near the apex, and a narrower stripe along the outer margin, being somewhat shorter than the sutural one, and running for its apical third at a little distance from the outer margin; beneath dark purple-brown, legs red.

Head closely punctured, with a small narrow ridge in front; hairy. Prothorax subconvex, rather short, sides gently rounded, slightly narrowed towards the top; deeply punctured, rugosely at the sides, with an irregular glabrous line in the middle; hairy. Elytra rather short, gradually narrowed towards the top, apices moderately divergent, sutural and marginal spines rather broad and short, the humeral fold small, angularly produced; costate, interstices plain, slightly transversely wrinkled, with a distinct row of shallow punctures on each. Undersurface very closely and finely punctured; covered, legs included, with a delicate silvery pubescence.

Unique in coll. Oberthür.

13. Astraeus Oberthüri v. d. Poll. — nov. spec.

Elongatus, nitidus, supra purpureo-brunneus, in elytris fulgentius; singula elytra fascia obliqua ab humero ad suturam ante medium, macula basali et tribus maculis in parte apicali, flavis notata; subtus aureo-cupreus. Caput dense punctatum. Prothorax convexus, lateribus apicem versus modice rotundato-angustatis; fortiter punctatus, creberrime in lateribus. Elytra costata, interstitiis planis, distincte sparsimque punctatis; apicibus sat divergentibus, spinis suturalibus et marginalibus subacutis. Pars infera confertim punctata, densissime subtilissimeque in abdomine. Caput, thorax et pars infera pubescentia sericea tecta, densius subtus.

Long. 9—10$\frac{1}{2}$ mm., lat. 3$\frac{1}{2}$—4 mm.

Habitat: Australia.

Shining, uppersurface purple-brown, the elytra more brilliant; each of the elytra with a flavous spot at the base, a strongly curved band, originating at the shoulder and extending to the suture somewhat above the middle, without touching, however, the suture, its concavity turned towards the base, a row of three spots, of which the first is situated almost in the middle at the outer margin, the third near the suture at some distance from the top, the second midway between the first and third, moreover a very small punctiform spot close to the suture and midway between the fascia and the apical spot. Underneath and legs golden coppery.

Head thickly punctured; hairy. Prothorax convex, sides rounded, moderately narrowed anteriorly; deeply punctured, chiefly at the sides; hairy, Elytra gradually narrowed towards the top, apices slightly divergent, apical and marginal spines strong, the humeral fold angularly produced; costate, interstices plain, faintly plicated, with a row of distant deep punctures on each. Undersurface closely punctate, more finely and densely on the abdomen; clothed, legs included, with a sparse silvery pile.

Variability. The punctiform spots near the suture disappear, and the fascia has a tendency to become separated into two spots. Two specimens in coll. Oberthür. Dedicated to Mr. R. Oberthür.

14. Astraeus elongatus v. d. Poll.

Astraeus elongatus v. d. Poll, *Not. from the Leyd. Mus.*, VIII (1886), p. 177.

Elongatus, parallelus, nitidus. Caput aureo-viride ut et prothorax in medio cyanescens vel nigrescens; elytra atro-coerulea, violaceo-internitentia, singula elytra septenis maculis flavis notata; pars infera cum pedibus laete viridis, nitidissima. Caput crassum, fronte profunde, vertice sparsim punctatum. Prothorax convexus, lateribus subrotundatis, apicem versus fere haud angustatis; fortiter punctatus, subtilius in disco. Elytra costata, interstitiis planis, punctis magnis fere confluentibus instructis; pro magna parte parallela, apicibus mediocriter divergentibus, spinis suturalibus lateralibusque acutis. Pars infera confertim punctata, in abdomine subtilius sed densissime; pubescentia minutissima sericea induta.

Long. $9\frac{1}{2}$—12 mm., lat. 3—$4\frac{1}{2}$ mm.

Habitat: Queensland, West Australia, Port Denison, Swan River.

Shining. Head golden-green, the vertex cyaneous or violaceous-black. Thorax golden-green on the disc, the sides more golden, the base and the median lobe blackish or purplish. Elytra black with cyaneous or violaceous reflections, each of them ornated with a row of four yellow spots along the suture, the first at the base, the second before the middle, the third below the middle, the fourth midway between the foregoing and the apex, and a row of three spots at the outer margin, their position corresponding with the intervals between the sutural spots, the third one always at a little distance from the margin. Underneath and legs golden-green.

Head large, swollen, deeply punctured, more sparsely on the vertex, which is slightly furrowed; hairy. Prothorax convex, sides slightly rounded and somewhat narrowed towards the top, the front-margin slightly produced in the centre, narrowly margined along the front and the sides; strongly punctured, rugosely at the sides; hairy. Elytra parallel-sided, suddenly narrowed below the middle towards the apex, apices moderately divergent, sutural and marginal spines strong, but short, the humeral fold rather small, somewhat angularly produced; costate, interstices plain, slightly wrinkled in a transverse direction, each with a row of closely set punctures. Beneath densely punctured, the abdomen very thickly and minutely; clothed with a very delicate silvery pile.

Variability. This seems to be a pretty constant species, for although I have seen a good number of specimens, I could not find any noticeable variety; there is only a tendency of the second sutural spot to flow together with the humeral spot.

Number of specimens examined: seven, in coll. Oberthür and van de Poll.

15. Astraeus simulator v. d. Poll. — nov. spec.

Elongatus, nitidus; capite prothoraceque obscure viridi-aeneis, purpurascentibus; elytris atro-coeruleis, singulis elytris ad basin macula magna, ante et post medium fascia lata, ante apicem macula parva, flava ornatis; subtus cum pedibus viridi-aeneus; apices tibiarum et articuli duo priores tarsorum testacei. Caput dense punctatum, in medio longitudinaliter leviter impressum. Prothorax sat brevis, convexus, lateribus rotundato-angustatis apicem versus; fortiter punctatus, creberrime in lateribus. Elytra costata, interstitiis planis, subtiliter punctatis et plicatis; apicibus valde divergentibus, spinis suturalibus marginalibusque longis, acutis. Pars infera confertim punctata; caput, prothorax et pars infera pubescentia minutissima sericea obtecta.

Long. 7 mm., lat. 2½ mm.

Habitat: Peak Downs.

Shining, head bronzy-green in front, purple-brown on the vertex, prothorax bronzy-green with the sides purple-brown, elytra cyaneous-black, each with a large yellow spot at the base, a broad fascia before the middle, originating below the shoulder and not quite reaching the suture, an other broad fascia below the middle, also touching the outer margin only, and a punctiform spot close to the apex; underneath metallic green with violaceous reflections, legs green with the tip of the tibiae and the two first tarsal joints testaceous.

Head strongly punctured, slightly longitudinally excavated in the middle; hairy. Prothorax convex, sides rounded and moderately narrowed towards the top, with a narrow margin along the front and the sides; coarsely punctured, rugose at the sides; hairy. Elytra gradually narrowed towards the top, apices rather strongly divergent, sutural and marginal spines long and acute, the humeral fold large and very acutely produced; costate, interstices plain, slightly transversely plicated, with a row of shallow punctures on each. Undersurface densely punctured, clothed with a very minute silvery pile.

This species is very nearly allied to *A. pygmaeus* v. d. Poll var. *subfasciatus* mihi, but besides by the presence of the additional small spot before the apex and the apical fascia, replacing the apical spot, which does never touche the margin in the latter, it differs essentially by the following structural characters, viz. the head has no frontal carina, the thorax is less narrowed towards the top, the humeral fold is more strongly produced.

Unique in my own collection.

16. Astraeus pygmaeus v. d. Poll.

Astraeus pygmaeus v. d. Poll, *Not. from the Leyd. Mus.*, VIII (1886), p. 178.

Elongatus, nitidus, supra coeruleus, violaceo-internitens (caput ut et prothorax interdum viridi-aeneum), singulis elytris maculis quaternis flavis ornatis; subtus cum pedibus laete violaceus vel cyaneus, apices tibiarum et articuli priores tarsorum testacei. Caput fortiter punctatum, in fronte carina longitudinali. Prothorax convexus, lateribus rotundatis et valde angustatis apicem versus, profunde punctatus, densius ad latera. Elytra costata, interstitiis planis, leviter punctatis et plicatis; apicibus valde divergentibus, spinis suturalibus lateralibusque validis, acutis. Pars infera dense punctata. Omnino, elytris exceptis, pubescentia minutissima sericea induta.

var. *subfasciatus* v. d. Poll, *a typo differt macula flava posthumerali cum macula secunda suturali confluente.*

Long. 5½—7 mm., lat. 2—3 mm.

Habitat: Queensland, Rockhampton, N. S. Wales, Port Denison, Wide Bay.

Shining, head blue or green in front, purple-brown on the vertex; prothorax entirely violaceous or blue on the disc and green at the sides, elytra cyaneous or bronzy-black, each with four flavous spots, the first at the base, the second close to the suture before the middle, the third below the shoulder and the fourth below the middle touching neither the suture nor the outer margin; beneath and legs cyaneous or violaceous, the tip of the tibiae and the first joint of the tarsi testaceous.

Head strongly punctured, with a strong longitudinal ridge in front, which is rather broad above the epistoma and diminishes gradually near the vertex; hairy. Prothorax convex, sides strongly rounded and narrowed towards the top, with a narrow margin along the front and the sides; deeply punctured on the disc, more coarsely at the sides; hairy. Elytra gradually narrowed towards the top, apices rather strongly divergent, sutural and lateral spines long and acute, the humeral fold moderately large and acutely produced; costate, interstices plain, feebly transversely wrinkled, each with a row of distant punctures. Underneath coarsely punctate, the abdomen more shallowly; clothed with an extremely delicate silvery pile.

Variability. The second sutural spot is often confluent with the humeral spot, effecting a transverse band (var. *subfasciatus* m.).

Number of specimens examined: thirteen, in coll. Oberthür and van de Poll.

17. Astraeus dilutipes v. d. Poll. — nov. spec.

Astraeus Samouelli Saund., var. *dilutipes* v. d. Poll, *Not. from the Leyd. Mus.*, VIII (1886), p. 180 footnote.

Elongatus, nitidus; supra atro-coerulens, violaceo-internitens, capite prothoraceque viridi-aenescentibus; elytris singulis maculis quintenis flavis ornatis; subtus viridi-aeneus, cyaneo- vel violaceo-internitens, pedibus prorsus testaceis, tarsis sub-nigrescentibus. Caput fortiter punctatum, in fronte linea elevata glabra. Prothorax convexus, lateribus apicem versus rotundato-angustatis; fortiter aequaliterque punctatus, in medio impressione laevi longitudinali. Elytra costata, interstitiis planis, leviter punctatis et plicatis; apicibus valde divergentibus, spinis suturalibus marginalibusque validis, acutis. Pars infera confertim punctata, subtilius in abdomine. Omnino, elytris exceptis, pubescentia minutissima sericea tecta.

Long. 8½—10 mm., lat. 3—4 mm.

Habitat: N. S. Wales, Wide-Bay.

Shining, head aeneous-green with purplish reflections in front and on the vertex in the female; golden green with the vertex purple-brown in the male. Prothorax dark aeneous-green mingled with purplish-brown, chiefly at the sides, in the female; in the male the thorax is divided in a transverse direction by an angular ∧∧-shaped line, the greater basal part being obscure bronzy-green, the smaller upperpart golden-green, whilst the line of demarcation between the two portions is bright coppery. Elytra cyaneous-black, each with a yellow spot just at the base, two spots before the middle placed abreast, the exterior one below the shoulder, the other one near the suture, a small band below the middle, touching the outer margin only and a spot close to the apex. Beneath green with blue and violaceous tinges; legs entirely testaceous, the last tarsal joints blackish.

Head very closely punctured, with a rather strong longitudinal ridge in front; hairy. Antennae very long, chiefly in the male sex. Prothorax convex, sides rounded and rather strongly narrowed towards the top, slightly margined along the front and the sides; deeply and regularly punctured, with a feebly impressed dorsal line; hairy. Elytra gradually narrowed towards the top, apices moderately divergent, sutural and marginal spines strong and acute, the humeral fold middle-sized, acutely produced; costate, interstices plain, slightly transversely wrinkled, with a row of closely set small punctures on each. Undersurface coarsely punctured, the abdomen more thickly and finely; clothed with a minute silvery pubescence.

This species is very closely allied to the next following *A. Samouelli* Saund., and in my former paper on the genus, when having but a single specimen at my disposal, I only considered it a variety of *Samouelli* with entirely testaceous legs. Disposing now of a larger material, I find the following principal differences, viz. the general shape is more slender; the distribution of the colors on the thorax in the male is quite different; the humeral spot is not composed of two confluent spots; there is no punctiform yellow spot at the base in the shoulder edge.

Variability. The humeral and the second sutural spots have a tendency to become confluent, but even in the specimen, where they are almost united, there is no trace of the third spot, which is always present in *Samouelli*. The thighs, chiefly of the hinder legs, are sometimes partly bluish.

Number of specimens examined: four, in coll. Oberthür and van de Poll.

18. Astraeus Samouelli Saund.

Stigmodera Samouelli Hope, Buprestidae, (1836), p. 6, (unpublished tract).

Astraeus Samouelli Saund., Trans. Ent. Soc. Lond., 1868, p. 10, pl. 1, fig. 12.

Astraeus Samouelli v. d. Poll, Not. from the Leyd. Mus., VIII (1886), p. 180.

Praecedenti valde similis sed praecipue differt: statura robustiore; macula perparva in sinu humerali; macula posthumerali duabus maculis confluentibus composita. Eodem colore ac dilutipes sed caput prothoracisque latera splendiora cuprea et viridi-aurea; pedes cyanei, apicibus tibiarum et articulis primis tarsorum testaceis.

var. Mastersi Mc. Leay, A typo differt, macula flava posthumerali cum macula secunda sub-suturali confluente.

Long. 8½—10 mm., lat. 3½—4½ mm.

Habitat: N. S. Wales.

Shining, head bright green in front and purple-brown on the vertex; in the female, bright golden with the vertex coppery in the male; prothorax purple-brown with the sides bright green in the female, dark coppery with golden green sides and indefinite purple-brown patches at the base near the median lobe in the male; elytra black, with cyaneous or purple reflections, each with six yellow markings, a spot just at the base, an other one before the middle close to the suture, a very small punctiform spot in the shoulder edge, a large irregular spot (properly composed of two spots, which is evident in one of my specimens, where they are separated on the left elytron) below the shoulder, a small fascia below the middle, which reaches the outer margin only, and a spot midway between the apex and the fascia. Underside and legs green, cyaneous or violaceous; tips of the tibiae and the first joint of the tarsi testaceous.

Head closely punctured, with an elevated median line in front; hairy. Antennae very long, chiefly in the male sex. Prothorax convex, the front-margin slightly produced in the middle, sides rounded and rather strongly narrowed towards the top, narrowly

margined along the front and the sides; deeply but not closely
punctured, the punctures becoming larger at the sides, with a
faintly impressed median line; hairy. Elytra gradually narrowed
towards the apex, apices strongly divergent, sutural and marginal
. spines long and acute, the humeral fold large and acutely produced;
costate, interstices plain, moderately transversely wrinkled, each
with a row of large distant punctures. Undersurface coarsely
punctured, the abdomen more finely; clothed with an extremely
delicate silvery pubescence.

Variability. The irregular spot below the shoulder is often
confluent with the spot near the suture, forming a somewhat
zigzag-shaped band (var. *Mastersi* Mc. L.); the fascia below the
middle is sometimes interrupted and in some specimens there are
small punctiform additional spots almost in the middle close to
the suture.

Number of specimens examined: four of each sex (all the males
which have come under my notice belong to the var. *Mastersi*),
in coll. Oberthür and van de Poll.

19. Astraeus splendens v. d. Poll. — nov. spec.

*Elongatus, nitidus, caput laete cupreum; prothorax lateraliter
viridis, ad basin atro-purpureus, caeterum laete cupreus; elytra
atro-coerulea, singula elytra ad basin magna, ante medium fascia
lata, post medium fascia breviore et ante apicem macula parva,
flava ornata. Subtus cum pedibus dilute viridi-aureus, apice tibiarum
et articulo primo tarsorum testaceis. Caput crebre punctatum, in
fronte linea elevata glabra. Prothorax convexus, lateribus apicem
versus rotundato-angustatis, crebre punctatus, subtilius in disco, in
medio longitudinaliter paululum impressus. Elytra costata, interstitiis
planis, distincte punctatis, leviter plicatis; apicibus valde divergentibus, spinis suturalibus lateralibusque validis, acutis. Pars
infera confertim punctata, in abdomine subtilius. Omnino, elytris
exceptis, pubescentia subtilissima sericea induta.*

*Varietati « M a s t e r s i Mc. L. » proxima, sed facile distinguenda
appendice humerali multo longiore et angulatiore.*

Long. 8—9 mm., lat. 3—3½ mm.

Habitat: Rockhampton.

Shining, head and thorax brilliant golden-coppery, the latter with the sides broadly golden-green and with a purple-black heart-shaped patch on the disc before the median lobe; elytra black with cyaneous or violaceous reflections, each with a large flavous spot at the base, a broad fascia before the middle originating at the shoulder and not quite reaching the suture, an other smaller fascia below the middle also reaching the outer margin only, and a spot midway between the band and the apex. Underside and legs bright bluish-green, in the middle golden-green; tips of the tibiae and two first joints of the tarsi testaceous.

Head densely punctured, with an elevated median line in front; hairy. Antennae very long, chiefly in the male sex. Prothorax convex, sides rounded and rather strongly narrowed towards the top, narrowly margined along the sides and the front, which is slightly prominent in the middle; deeply and closely punctured, with a faintly impressed line in the centre; hairy. Elytra gradually narrowed towards the top, apices rather strongly divergent, sutural and lateral spines long and acute, the humeral fold very long and strongly acutely produced; costate, interstices plain, slightly transversely wrinkled, each with a row of large shallow punctures. Underneath coarsely punctured, somewhat more finely on the abdomen; clothed with a delicate silvery pile.

This species is nearly allied to the var. *Mastersi* Mc. L. of *A. Samouelli* Saund., but differs by its smaller size, more brilliant color of head and thorax, proportionately broader yellow markings and much larger humeral fold.

Variability. The spots before the apex disappear.

Number of specimens examined: five, in coll. Oberthür and van de Poll.

EXPLANATION OF PLATE II AND III.

Fig. 1. *Astraeus irregularis* v. d. Poll.
   1 *a.* side view of the elytron.
  2. *Astraeus lineatus* v. d. Poll.
   2 *a.* side view of the elytron.
  3. *Astraeus multinotatus* v. d. Poll.
   3 *a.* side view of the elytron.
  4. *Astraeus aberrans* v. d. Poll.
   4 *a.* side view of the elytron.
  5. *Astraeus navarchis* Thoms.
   5 *a.* side view of the elytron.
  6. *Astraeus fraterculus* v. d. Poll.
   6 *a.* side view of the elytron.
  7. *Astraeus Badeni* v. d. Poll.
   7 *a.* side view of the elytron.
  8. *Astraeus Jansoni* v. d. Poll.
   8 *a.* side view of the elytron.
  9. *Astraeus crassus* v. d. Poll.
   9 *a.* side view of the elytron.
  10. *Astraeus flavopictus* Cast. et Gory.
   10 *a.* side view of the elytron.
  11. *Astraeus prothoracicus* v. d. Poll.
   11 *a.* side view of the elytron.
  12. *Astraeus vittatus* v. d. Poll.
   12 *a.* side view of the elytron.
  13. *Astraeus Oberthüri* v. d. Poll.
   13 *a.* side view of the elytron.
  14. *Astraeus elongatus* v. d. Poll.
   14 *a.* side view of the elytron.
  15. *Astraeus simulator* v. d. Poll.
   15 *a.* side view of the elytron.
   15 *b.* detail of the head.
  16. *Astraeus pygmaeus* v. d. Poll.
   16 *a.* side view of the elytron.
   16 *b.* elytron of the var. *subfasciatus* v. d. Poll.
   16 *c.* detail of the head.
  17. *Astraeus dilutipes* v. d. Poll.
   17 *a.* side view of the elytron.
  18. *Astraeus Samouelli* Saund.
   18 *a.* side view of the elytron.
   18 *b.* elytron of the var. *Mastersi* Mac Leay.
  19. *Astraeus splendens* v. d. Poll.
   19 *a.* side view of the elytron.

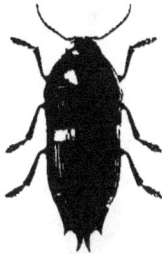

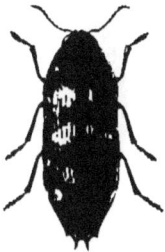

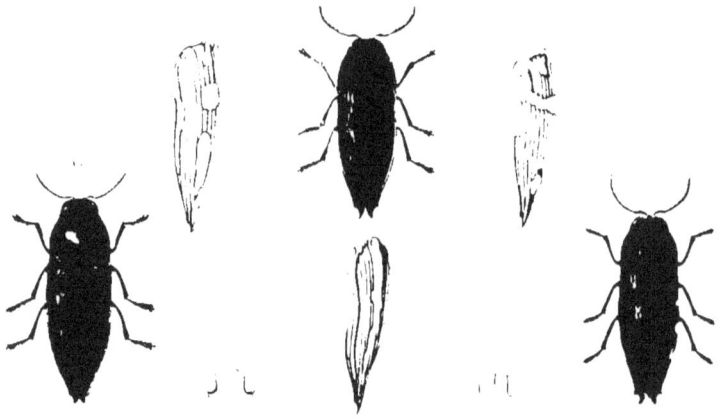

www.ingramcontent.com/pod-product-compliance
Lightning Source LLC
Chambersburg PA
CBHW021605270326
41931CB00009B/1377